Poems from a Grateful Heart On Turning 80

ISBN: 9781796684940

FRM Publishing
6801 Brookeshire Dr. Suite 101
West Bloomfield, Michigan 48322
Email: Faye@frmpublishing.com
Website: FRMpublishing.com

Printed in the U.S.A.

Personal Note

I began writing poetry post-retirement several years ago, inspired by a wonderful teacher and poet, Catherine Mahoney, to whose memory one of my poems is dedicated. I am not a poet; I write poems as others garden flowers - for the sheer beauty and surprise of it - surprise in the sense of you never know what you're going to get. I seek no plaudits for my poems, and am too crotchety for criticism - though surely in need of it for improvement. I tender this small book of poems to family and friends - old and new - in gratitude for the lovely times we have spent together, and hope you derive some pleasure from reading them.

Joel

Acknowledgements

Much thanks to Faye Menczer Ascher for her patience, acumen, and guidance in composing this book and bringing it to fruition. Self-publishing is a stressful adventure for the novice, but Faye made it a happy journey. Also thanks to my IRP poetry group for deepening my love and appreciation of poetry.

TO MARGARET

It is beautiful ... there is no other purpose than the beauty of it. And that is reason enough to be.

Donald Hall
U.S. Poet Laureate

TABLE OF POEMS

DOCENT DAUGHTER

Nearly the same age as her story-telling
mother, Celia, who left this world
   all too soon
to tell stories in another realm
of Vilna, Pinsk and Chelm
where Marc and Bella* embraced
in the Sabbath-scented air.

Same piercing dark brown eyes
same passionate intensity.

The beautiful art loving docent daughter
my wife of 50 years
in a room of ancient Middle East artifacts
dressed all in black
a silver three-ringed necklace
lovely around her neck
told our small group of studious friends

*Mark Chagall and his wife Bella

In this great ceramic wall panel we see
the fierce Snake Dragon of Marduk
patron god of ancient Babylon.

Note the deadly fangs, scorpion tail, grasping talons
2500 years ago when Jews lived in the city of Babylon
this terrible creature guarded the gate to the palace
warning all who entered that the King of Babylon
was the mightiest ruler under the sun.

We shrank as the dragon bowed slightly
for a job well done.

GETTING READY

As I gazed out the window
at my wife's flower garden
beginning to fade
at summer's end
my eye caught
in the elbow of a locust tree
not five feet away
a small squirrel
munching on a nut

or was it the flesh
of a sugar pear?

turning the object
with its tiny paws
for the choicest bite
savoring a delicacy
of summer's bounty
storing fat
for the leaner months
of autumn and winter
lying just ahead.

AUTUMN

The sun slowly tugs summer into fall
when flowers drop their faded petals
and bullfrogs no longer croak
in the wetland pond.

Where today the white egret stands -
her mate of last summer - gone
I thought him faithful as a swan
perfidy or death - no one can say
but she feeds alone in the pond today.

Trees welcome autumn's coming
painting their leaves in brilliant hues
reigning supreme in beauty's eye
till they die at winter's icy hand.

But autumn's no harbinger
of wintery blight
it's a time to pause
and set things right
to comfort and heal
the troubled soul
cooling spring's ardor
and summer's heat
into reflection and grace
if we let it.

WINTER

Six weeks into winter
first snowfall
tiny flakes
coating everything in sight
twigs, bushes, stems
from last year's growth
no pointillist
could be so exacting.

Last fall we burlapped
our small Hydrangea plants
to protect them from winter freeze
placed stakes on four sides
swaddling them with burlap
with a swatch of burlap
over the top
like a small roof.

As the snow grew heavier the
roof sagged from the weight.

From our backyard kitchen window
the burlapped plants looked like
tiny dilapidated Japanese houses
in a winter landscape.

Behind them an old wood stake fence
with missing teeth.

The snow was pristine
dead maple leaves
skidded over the top
at the slightest breeze
no footprint of squirrel
or bird marred the surface.

Night now
Not a sound
All pristine white.

> *Winter solitude -*
> *in a world of one color*
> *the sound of the wind*
>
> Matsuo Basho (1644-1694)

OLD AGE

Before she died at 93
My mother turned and said to me
Age is just a number -
But I disagree
Numbers are hard things - no more, no less
But old age is more like the sea
An intimation of eternity.

Where's my glasses?
I need them to find things I cannot see
I put them there before I woke
To eat a peach and smell a rose.

Look within for things you need to find
No glasses needed for that task
But if your treasure you falsely suppose
    lies in the world
Your glasses are perched upon your nose.

When we die we decompose
Into atoms and things
Smaller than they
Quarks and leptons
Our scientists say.

But my spirit I believe
Is more like the sea
To dance among the stars
For eternity.

ALAS POOR VERSE

Poetry is hard
verse is worse
a poet's allure
is a versifier's curse

in certain poetic corners
rhyme is suspect
if it ends a line
or isn't sublime, and

verses with the meter
of a nursery rhyme
are a telling sign
of a jejune mind

so Jack and Jill went up a hill
and Jack Sprat
abhorred all fat

what is that to poets of serious incline
who serve readers inscrutable fare
some find exotic and thrilling
and others disdain as hot air?

but on one thing both agree
poetry's a solemn affair.

Should we care?

must poetry be cheerless and dreary?

"Yes" and "no" I answer the questions
and ask the guardians of poetry's estate
will "Whimsy" and "Nonsense" be admitted
or must they stand beggars at Poetry's gate?

and if the answer is no - go away
arrant versifiers like you are unwelcome
I'll persist in pressing my case

what about Ogden, surname Nash
who denied the existence
of three L-lllamas
bringing smiles to every reader's face?

and Charles Lutwidge Dodgson
a/k/a Lewis Carroll
who loved a little girl
named Alice Liddell
and made her adventures
childhood's greatest tale?

do you think poets like these
in the contemporary scene
could get their poems published
in *Poetry* magazine?*

silly question, of course
and we're all the poorer for that.

Poetry is an elite magazine founded in 1912. The
conceit of "Alas" is that "verse" as described in the
poem – no matter how good – would be rejected
today by *Poetry* for lack of gravitas.

LUCA DELLA ROBBIA'S "MAKE A JOYFUL NOISE" AT THE DETROIT INSTITUTE OF ARTS

Young maidens in diaphanous gowns
Fingers interlaced
Whirling in dance
Hands aloft
Supporting gigantic trumpets
Blown by bulging - cheeked young men

All carved from a single slab of marble
Poetry in stone
To melt the adamant heart.*

*Best read while viewing a clear image of the work
- readily available online.

THANKSGIVING

I

Not your Norman Rockwell golden-brown bird
waiting to be carved at the Thanksgiving table
but two large, dark, scrawny, wild turkeys
zigzagging across our backyard lawn this morning
pecking for - God knows what in the snow scattered half
frozen ground
until they turkey-trotted out of sight.
These I imagined were the tough, undomesticated birds
Pilgrims ate with native Americans
at the first Thanksgiving.

II

Native Americans were here first
but millions came after them - some in chains -
and it is the humble American turkey that holds
the place of honor at the great national holiday
of freedom proclaimed by Lincoln
that unites all Americans.

III
We all come from somewhere else –
we are all immigrants

Give me your tired, your poor,
Your huddled masses yearning
to breathe free

Lincoln and Emma Lazarus
Kentucky - born farmer's son
and descendant of Spanish Jews
they are the glory of this country.

The lamp held aloft still shines as a
beacon of liberty and opportunity
to oppressed peoples all over the world.

And in time - when the better angels
of our nature take hold - if we will it so –
America will reclaim its place
*as the last best hope of earth.**

* Lincoln's 1862 *State of the Union Address.*

14

ELLIS' FIRST HAIRCUT

I went to Great Clips this morning
for my bimonthly haircut
Tuesday $9.99 seniors special
looking like Bernie Sanders on a bad hair day.

There I saw a little boy sitting on his
mother's lap in a barber chair
golden curls encircling his angelic face
androgynous beauty - prompting one to ask
"Little boy or little girl?"
turned one year old two days ago.

A young blond-haired dad, dressed in cargo pants,
Dracula T-shirt, and high school jacket lettered
"2014 Wrestling Team District Champs"
hovered nearby, camera in hand.

The hairdresser went to work circling
the wide-eyed child squirming on his mother's lap
lopping golden curls and snipping wayward locks
and when the task was completed to near perfection
there emerged before his parents' adoring eyes –
a little boy - no longer babe - named Ellis
to make his way in the world.

Great Clips presents parents with a snippet of hair
from their child's first haircut
placing it in a small envelope
for safe keeping.

Over the years the envelope might be lost
        or forgotten
but so great was the love I witnessed that day,
and so tenacious our precious memories lay
I would not be surprised if on Ellis' wedding day
his mother took the snippet of hair
from the envelope
and pressed it to her lips.

LAUGHING MAN

December.
Driving back to Michigan
from visiting my son in Indiana.
bone chilling cold
temperature near zero
dreary, sunless day.

Gusts of icy snow makes driving treacherous.
makes me think of opening lines
of Frost's poem "Fire and Ice"

> *Some say the world will end in fire,*
> *Some say in ice.*

Wondering if ice would be my demise.

Pulled into first rest stop in Michigan
across the Ohio border.

Outside the restrooms a short rotund man was hunched over
mopping the snow-wet floor.

"Careful of the wet floor," he said.
"Thanks, I will," I said, as I entered the bathroom.
A few moments later, I heard rollicking laughter
coming from outside the bathroom door
the strangest sound at a place like that.

As I left the bathroom, the man's eye caught mine
a huge grin on his face.

"What makes you so happy on a day like this?"
    I asked.
"I'm happy every day."
"Do you like your job?"
"I love it!" he said.
"Been at the floors 27 years, every day
I make people laugh."

Made me laugh too
His infectious joy
A gift of grace
In the unlikeliest place.

MORNING IN EDEN

Trouble sleeping
comes with age
woke up at 5:00 a.m.
headed to back bedroom to do some reading
on the way I glanced out the front window
dark, raining - lawn dimly lit by floodlight.

On the lawn I saw two strange large forms
side by side - still as monoliths
I stared until the stillness was
broken by a flicker of white
and they vanished into the mist.

I returned to our bedroom
and softly woke my sleeping wife.

"They're back," I said
"Who?" she asked drowsily
"The deer who browsed at dawn
on the first shoots of spring
in your garden
Oh how furious you were!"

"I'm not angry anymore," she murmured
"they were so graceful and beautiful,"
She closed her eyes
and fell back to sleep.

And so I think it must have been
on the sixth day of creation.

Adam up early and restless
to watch over his domain
Eve newborn blissfully asleep
dreaming of her lovely garden
deer forever browsing
in the miracle of creation.

OUR CHOICE

We only live once on this earthly sphere
some believe another lies in store
maybe - but no confirming text yet -
if you lack a smart phone, call collect.

So here's the question:
in our blink of time
what are we going to do?

Pleasure is all
grab all that you can
some hold that philosophy.

Others say that's bunk
and I agree
there's no true happiness
where all is me.

Feed the hungry
care for the poor,
widow, orphan and stranger
are they not our kin too?
(if you say nay - check your DNA.)

The choice is ours
we can't eschew
 so what are you and I
 gonna do?

MAY IN MICHIGAN

One of those great Michigan May afternoons.

Last week three deer nibbled on the first shoots of
Spring in the back yard garden my wife lovingly
Tends like a new born babe.

"Be gone," she shouted, half wishing they'd stay
So beautiful they were on a lovely spring day.

Today the first purple iris stood erect and proud
Like a haughty king.
Soon others of variegated hue will join his court
To sway in praise and sip the morning dew.

But not all things flourish in nature's bounty
Affluence at times yields only a few.

Tiny maple seeds carpet our black asphalt drive
Twirling in thousands from a mothering tree
   to infertile ground
Where they must die, bereft of soil and rain.

But only one need thrive, by chance or design,
Fallen on soil and nourished by rain
For the mothering tree to lovingly say
Live sweet child for another spring day.

WETLAND PRESERVE
(In memory of Catherine Mahony*)

There is a small wetland preserve in the middle
    of our Detroit suburb
Fed by the overflow of a tributary to the Rouge river.

It is hidden from roving eyes by a short access road
But some of us know where it is.

A sign says "park open from dawn to dusk".
Wetland creatures are oblivious
Some humans too
Moonlight rebels free as wind and rain.

But beware small creatures
mouse, bunny, and vole
Ring-tailed masked hunters
Hunger for prey at night
So huddle in your burrows
Till break of day.

Four summers ago a cluster of milkweeds
Nursed a colony of monarch butterflies
in our wetland preserve.

And then they were gone.

Mowed down by wetland caretakers
Or snatched away by careless hands
The milkweeds were gone
The monarchs too
And the land was desolate
As Ezekiel knew.

Today I walked the wetland paths
Summer wildflowers everywhere,
But butterflies few.

Then as I turned a bend my heart stood still
There I saw a small cluster of milkweeds
Their pods tipped with droplets of white

And I knew.

And soon monarchs will know
That their small patch of heaven
Thrives anew
And their silent beauty
Will again make hearts
Burst into song.

Poet, teacher, muse.

THE OPEN SEA

Between the two halves of our lovely by-the-week
summer rental home - formerly a small two story
hotel the color of an orange
that would have been spectacular
on a bluff in Crete
overlooking the Sea

there stands a brick planter
about three feet high, two feet deep
lushly planted with
marigolds, snapdragons, and greens
watered by the rains
and a caretaker we never see.

The planter attracts little attention
ignored in the welter of beach
chairs, umbrellas, rubber rafts
and kids scampering between the two households
preparing for a day at the beach of Lake Michigan
across the street - down a short road.

For years the planter has been a thing of silent beauty
undisturbed except for an occasional ruffling in
search of a lost tennis ball.

But not today.

Around 9 a.m. as I was standing on the front porch,
looking to see if the beach flag was green,
signaling a safe swim day
out of the planter, a few feet away,
burst a full size brown duck
flapping to the pavement below.

You could have knocked me over with a feather!
But wait - there's more!

Seconds later nine tiny tufts of brown fuzz
each no bigger than a walnut
with legs skinny as toothpicks
culminating in pink webbed feet
the size of a grain of rice
tumbled out of the planter
to the hard pavement below.

The tiny creatures could not have been
ten minutes out of shell, but the impatient
mom showed them no solicitude,
promptly honking them to order,
and they followed her in a wobbly line
one behind the other - onto the green
grass of the still dewy front lawn.

And thus began an adventure
that would have daunted an Odysseus.
Ducklings need water - NOW! - to survive.
Across the road were tons of water
in vast Lake Michigan
but before getting there
there was a busy street to cross
and a wide sandy beach
with voracious sea gulls
and early morning beach goers
who would harry the little creatures to death.

The lake was out.

Behind the house - but still a long way off
about half a city block
was a channel from the lake
to the boat docks of the town.

The mom unhesitatingly headed in that direction
her brood trailing behind her
had she been there before?
probably - perhaps that's where she met the drake
that fathered her ducklings
or perhaps that's where her instincts led her
to find safety and food.

The journey, however, was not without great peril.
And to the reader faint of heart
you might want to put aside this poem
and return to the "Ten Little Ducklings"
of your childhood for a happy ending

WARNING: There's no telling how our adventure
          will turn out!

First the voyagers had to traverse
our backyard, a relatively safe journey
as I walked discretely behind them
to avert any harm.

They then had to cross under a wooden fence
into our neighbor's backyard -
a dangerous place for trespassers like us.

No one seemed to be at home
but a guarding dog
or pouncing cat
would have doomed
the hapless ducklings.
But none appeared.

An unimaginable terror, however, lay ahead.
At the far edge of the neighbor's property
demarcated by a rickety wooden fence
there was a precipice and wall at least
nine feet in height, descending to
concrete pavement below.

The mother duck reconnoitered the precipice twice
seeking a safe descent - but there was none.
So she flew down to the pavement below
where she issued a series of honks to her ducklings
huddled above.

And one by one, they leaped off the cliff
unaided by untested wings
they seemed like floating tufts of cotton
but their descent was swift in gravity's pull.

I closed my eyes at the horrific sight
then opened them reluctantly expecting
to see shattered bodies below.

But instead I saw nine valiant ducklings
struggling to their tiny feet - unharmed.
I could not believe my eyes, and when I saw
them safe, I imagined they had been escorted
by invisible angels in their miraculous descent.

I clambered down a flight of wooden steps to
the pavement to see the wondrous sight.

The channel was now less than twenty feet away
small boats and feeding ducks were in the water
a few fishermen on the bank.

The mother duck led her exhausted
ducklings to the edge of the channel.
She jumped in - and so did they - though they had
never known water before - and scarcely land.

In the water they gathered around her.
She showed them how to paddle and
bob for food.

And they set out as a family to the open sea.

HEAVEN AND EARTH

What is the worth of an untestable hypothesis?
To the scientist - zero.
To the imagination - pure gold.
Or am I being too bold
To suggest such dichotomy?

Does not science fly on the wings of imagination?
Can we leap to earth without venturing the sky?
Was Einstein's mind stocked with formulae?
Or was it a dream visited that led him to discover
that mass and energy are the
same as you and I?

Of course science is needed to expose falsity
Let loose and we are all undone
Wasting time spinning straw into gold
And fearing to step off the end of the earth
Unless caught by heaven below
Where Hell is thought to dwell.

So they must learn to live in harmony
imagination adorning the tree's tough bark
spirit soaring on a bed of steel
and life to live in commonweal.

AVI AT THE FARM

Even then Avi had a mind of his own
at age 3 he wanted to go to a farm
with his Sunday school class
to ride a tractor and milk a goat
suburban kid susceptible to rural fables -
mostly from stories in picture books
bottom line: Avi found the farm to be a big bore
tractor ride a bust - especially second time around
milking a goat - ick!
a little yank on the tit, and that was it
petting a turkey? - don't ask
turkeys are crazy birds who hate being petted
(and eaten).

Avi's major preoccupation was
confirming the existence
of farm animals from a check sheet
handed out by Farmer Judy
if it wasn't on the list - it didn't exist.
When I pointed out a pony
Avi said "no" it wasn't listed on the sheet
(of course it was - but his reading skills
weren't highly developed at that time)
this led to a heated argument on the tractor
loaded with 3 year olds and their adoring moms
best I can describe the dispute:
Avi's position was Talmudic, mine scientific.

By this time Avi was sick of the farm and me
"no" he said, he didn't want to see a bunny
just wanted to go home and get some orange juice.

He agreed to stick around for snacks
which consisted of milk and one crummy
graham cracker, which he rejected
probably on principle.

Avi was hungry and surly on the drive home
when he got home, he gulped down
a sippy-cup of orange juice.

His mom asked him: "How was the farm?"
Avi said, "Great"!

Go figure.

Ariel was glad he had written his poems.
They were of a remembered time or of
something seen that he liked.

Wallace Stevens

Made in the USA
Las Vegas, NV
20 April 2023

70851515R00024